The Sanity

Behind

Sanctification

Deirdre Avant

LOVE CLONES

publishing

Love Clones Publishing
www.lcpublishing.net

First Printing, 2015

ISBN: 978-0692379028

Publishers:

Love Clones Publishing

Dallas, TX

www.lcpublishing.net

ACKNOWLEDGMENTS

There are three groups of people that I would like to acknowledge who helped me bring this book to fruition. The first group is my family who has been there from the very beginning. This group taught me the fundamentals of life and did what they could to get me off to a great start. Without my family's support and love I would not be where I am today. There are so many thanks to all of them.

The second group is my friends some of whom I've known since grade school others came along through college, past jobs, and church. This group struggled with me, cried with me, celebrated with me and pushed me when necessary.

The last group is ministry leadership from spiritual parents, spiritual siblings, and co-laborers in the kingdom. This group helped me to grow spiritually in more ways than one. Some pushed so that I could see what I thought

DEDICATION

I dedicate this book to my deceased grandmother, Marian. In her latter years she really walked with the Lord in such a way that unfortunately, as a young person I could not appreciate it. I now know what she wanted me to realize and I can say I understand. My grandmother loved young people and it showed in her actions, even at her funeral the youth did a presentation because of the time she spent with them and the love she showed. Through her lifestyle, I was able to see what living a set apart life was like.

I am also thankful for two loving parents Robert and Viola who have always been in my corner. Life truly would not be possible without them – Love them both to life!

Last but definitely not least to my two sons, Brandon and Arion, who are my day-to-day reminders that God truly is in the blessing business.

I could not do and others ministered at appropriate times to help provide direction. All of these groups have played such a vital role in my life that I could not go without acknowledging them in my very first book.

INTRODUCTION

In the Sanity Behind Sanctification, it is my intent to make the process of sanctification plain and understandable. In the following chapters God will reveal His overall plans for purity. God is seeking a people who are sold out to Him and only Him. Rest assured when He returns He will be seeking a bride without a spot or wrinkle.

We should be glad that we are God's chosen generation, with whom He is well pleased. Do not take lightly the task you have ahead. Responsibility will weigh heavy on you and He will hold you accountable. This is my decree unto you.

On May 16, 2003 a prophetic word was given to me by Prophetess Curtis, which allowed me to be prepared for the huge task that is assigned to my life.

Prophetess Curtis said to me, "Prophetess Avant, I'm sitting here looking at your name and I heard God speaking. He is saying 'Avant,

Avant, Oh My Avant. You have been set apart for such a time as this. God is using you in the second Advent – the second coming of Christ to prepare the church – the one He is coming back for without a spot, blemish or wrinkle or any such thing. His Glory is resting upon your life even now. Saith the Spirit of Grace."

In this word the Lord speaks of me being instrumental as He is equipping many to prepare the people and part of that preparation is the process that we will discuss in this book.

The definition of the word sanctification is *(1) Consecration, Purification (2) The effect of consecration (a.) sanctification of heart and life.*[1]

The definition of the word sane is (1) proceeding from a sound mind rational (2) mentally sound especially able to anticipate and appraise the effect of ones actions (3) healthy in body wise.[1]

Sanctification is a progressive work of God in man that makes us free from sin and more like Christ in our lives.

The Process of Sanctification[2]

1. Slaves to sin (non-Christian)
2. Growing in Holiness (Christian life)
3. Perfect Holiness (death)

Three Stages of Sanctification[2]

Sanctification has a definite beginning at regeneration. The initial moral change is the first stage in sanctification. This change of ones primary love and primary desires occurs at the beginning of sanctification. Sanctification – growing in holiness.

1 Thes. 5:23, Heb 2:11 Christ, 1 Peter 1:2, Holy Spirit, John 17:17, 19 Truth

Sanctification increases throughout life.

We are to grow more in our righteousness. Just as in the past we used all our members to grow in sin, in Christ we are to use them to grow in holiness. We should seek daily to be like Christ. Heb. 12:14 reads, *Strive for the holiness without which no one can see the Lord.* James 1:22 says, *Be doers of the word, and not hearers only.* 1 Peter 1:15 edifies, Be Holy yourselves in all your conduct.

Further definitions of what sanctification, purification and consecration are.

Sanctification is completed at death (for our souls) and when the lord returns (our bodies) once Jesus returns he will give us new bodies. Then we will fully "bear the image of the man of Heaven"[3]

Purification – ceremonial or spiritual cleansing. The Mosaic Law prescribed purification rites for those ceremonially defiled by touching a corpse by contact with bodily discharges by childbirth and by leprosy. The mother of Jesus offered turtle doves and pigeons as a sacrifice in her ceremonial cleansing.[4]

Consecration – dedication to God's service. To dedicate or set apart for God's exclusive use.

Believers are encouraged to consecrate or sanctify themselves to God's service (2 Tim 2:21)[5]

Slaves To Sin

As a young girl I was taught right from wrong. I was raised in church and knew how to sit, be seen and not heard. I was taught to pray the Lord's prayer at bedtime and over my meals. Often times we can get into a routine and take on a form of godliness without fully being in relationship with God. So I prayed daily but did not have a relationship with Him. I did it out of habit not really seeking God or desiring to really know him.

Holiness unto God – prepare thyself.
Make all things new whole again.

In school, I was protected by a loving grandmother who made sure I understood what it was to be a God-fearing woman. Yet as a young person you are challenged daily with what you are being taught at home and what you are exposed to in school. One of the most tested areas seems to be fornication, sex without being married. Teenagers are extremely hormonal which may cause sex to become their primary focus. As a young person I was extremely sheltered and retained from things that would make someone else street smart. This left me exposed to some things that I wasn't taught. In 11th grade, I met a man who was much older than me but I opted to date him any way.

Needless to say it progressed into a full-blown relationship. Over time we became closer. I had a really good friend who said, "Dee I believe this individual is a drug dealer" but I didn't believe it. I have always been a bold person so I asked him directly and he lied, saying he dealt guns as if that was any better. In an odd way I felt relieved because this meant that the original information I had received had been wrong. I explained to my friend what he said and she said, "Ok if that's what you want to believe then go right ahead."

As time progressed, I began to notice things that didn't add up. These things lead me to my final recognition that he was indeed a drug dealer. Regrettably at this point, I was too far in to him to just walk away so I stayed and begged him to lead a different life hoping he would change, but his defense was always that selling drugs was all he knew to do.

The Lord gives you gifts without repentance and I had the gift of knowledge yet didn't know it. There are many times I will just know something. I explained to him one day that when they catch you, they would place him under the jail. I had no idea the network that he had and how far his reach was. We finally separated in my senior year of college because I married someone else. Years later I received a phone call that my former boyfriend was picked up from work by the Federal Marshalls and was on his way to jail. I was so distraught that day that I went home from work early. I knew it was the beginning of a journey that he would have to suffer through because of his decisions.

When it hit the papers it stated that he was the largest cocaine dealer on the Eastern Shore. My grandmother called me extremely upset and said let me read you the article and she asked if I knew about his behavior. I explained to her that he worked full-time and lived at home. I never owned up to the fact that I knew he was involved in drugs.

Be mindful of who and what you connect to; be wise about your decisions. Soul ties will have you connected to something that God never intended for your life. Anyone can make a bad decision and they may have to suffer the consequences but God forgives and you can begin again but the choice is yours. I am happy to say that this individual is out of prison and leading a different life. Understand when you choose to go against what God has directed in his commandments you will have alliance with something that could cause you harm.

During my marriage for whatever reason I

opted not to have a prayer life, which left me open to something that would cause me great heartache. The marriage started off wrong because of all the things that happened in the beginning. However, I believed that love would make the difference. It worked out well for a short period of time only to head down hill quickly. I was 21 years old and a recent graduate of college, newly married and pregnant with my first child. This was a lot of responsibility for a young person just starting out but that's where I was. I lacked financial discipline where my husband was much stronger in that area. We would often butt heads on financial decisions because he was disciplined and I wasn't. I didn't grow up in a house where a man made decisions, this was done by my grandmother and she did fine as far as I was concerned. Taking instructions from my husband was a great adjustment for me. This caused riffs in the relationship that I did not foresee. This is never an excuse but this is what was given when infidelity occurred.

My husband often stated that I never listened to him and I didn't follow his instructions. Not to mention I had physically changed after having Brandon. For him this was the main reason for him to commit adultery. My friend called me again and asked me did I think my husband was cheating. She said, "think about it every week he starts an argument around the same time so that by the weekend he can get out of the house and he knows you won't care because your angry." Even though this was truly the case, I did not believe that he was being unfaithful. Yet, she was right again.

My husband waited until he purchased a house before he came home one day and said you have sixty days to find somewhere to live. I thought, this cannot be happening to me. Nevertheless, it was real and I had to find an apartment quickly that I could afford on my own with student loans, daycare, and car payment and insurance. How was I going to do it bringing home $300 a week? I found an apartment for $490 a month which I just barley qualified for but we were accepted. My husband and I lived separated for an entire year with little to no communication. At the end of that year my husband finally broke the silence. He called and said, "Do you remember the lady that I worked with?" I told him yes and he stated that they had been in a relationship during our marriage. Shortly after he called she called and stated she wanted to speak with me in person. I let her come by and she explained many instances of how they planned to spend time together and how she was pregnant but lost the baby. She even went on to say she still loved my husband but if I wanted him she would let him go. My husband recognized her car at my place and wanted to come in to make her leave. He listened to what she had to say and they broke out in to an argument in the middle of my living room. He stayed for a while but left and she remained. I'd heard all I needed to hear and by this time it was three in the morning and I wanted to go to bed. She didn't want to leave and my husband wanted to come back and talk to me alone. She was so far gone that she really wanted me to hide her in my closet so that she could hear what he had to say to me. I told her absolutely not and that she would have to leave. My husband and I tried for a while after this incident to reconcile but I could not get past the infidelity. So we divorced and I was left with major trust issues. Often times life situations will propel you into a life of prayer.

In 2003 I began a prophetic course through PIT (Prophets In Training) With Apostle Stansbury. At that time I was still going out to clubs and had a live in boyfriend. One night while in class, Apostle Stansbury stood up and said he didn't like to see people violate their temples, primarily through sex outside of marriage. At this time I was definitely engaged in premarital sex. I pleaded to God, if you get me out of here tonight without calling me out specifically I will not live like this again. And He answered; once I left the class I went home and told my boyfriend we can't continue to live like this and I won't be having sex anymore. He said you can't do it and laughed I said to him I hear God saying, "go and sin no more". He said you won't do it. After some time had passed he figured I would give in so he began to set up situations to get me home alone in my room. He soon became more aggressive to the point where once I had to literally lay my hands on his penis and command him to stop. He was extremely agitated because he was now no longer aroused.

Once you come to the place where you have made up your mind to go with God but also that you want to be kept, you will be surprised how determined you become. Eventually that relationship completely ended. A few short years later I met another gentleman who asked me out and I figured this would be easy I've been alone with God for a while now and I should be strong. We went on a date and of course I invited him in and he wanted to kiss and hug. I tried it for a little while but quickly realized this was not the way to go, it didn't' last long.

Next came an African man and he was definitely a flirt and full of anxiety for sex. I tried a relationship a little while with him even though I knew from the onset that he wasn't the one. One night out of my loneliness I let him come over after 9 p.m., which was a mistake. I heard the Lord clearly say not to do it but I did it anyway. When he got there he asked me to change my clothes. Against my better judgment I did it. Then we went to lay down and he was all over the place. His body was heavy like lead. Finally it got to be too much for me and I used the power of God to put an end to this. I laid hands on him and prayed and his whole body went limp. He fell into a deep sleep for the rest of the night. When he got up to leave in the morning. I told him the Lord said not to let him in and he said, "You should have listened". That was the last time we had an encounter like that.

I share these situations to give you a

glimpse into a life, which was on its way through the sanctification and purity process. Often times we violate our bodies because we have a desire to please the flesh which can never be satisfied. You would think over time we would recognize this but at times the urges are so strong. You literally have become a slave to sin. Nevertheless, there is freedom on the horizon but there is a process that you will endure and if you finish the course the end product is something that God will be proud of.

GROWING IN HOLINESS

After I decided to really seek Christ and give myself over to him completely I began to grow in holiness. This began with my decision to make reading the bible a daily occurrence. Once I began to read the word daily I began to literally thirst and hunger after the word. I was not only reading the bible but other Christian teaching books because I was on a quest to get to know God more. My desire to have a meaningful relationship grew stronger. I went from not reading a verse per day to a chapter per day to reading the whole bible in a year. Now I'm reading the word in different ways each year. If you study the word daily it will literally be written on your heart. When it's needed it will come out.

The next thing that became a passion for me was prayer. In prayer, I began to seek the Holy Spirit because I was baptized for the second time at Great Bethel and when the altar workers took me to the receiving room I did not speak in tongues after they spent time with me.   This led me to believe there was something wrong with me. Thus during my prayer time I began to seek God out for the Holy Spirit. One day while on my knees in prayer when I went to speak in English, unknown tongues came out. After I had come to a place of complete repentance, it finally dawned on me that my actions were done in the presence of God. I broke and cried like a baby because it was at that point that I wanted to live to please God. Once that was released it was as if the Holy Spirit had an opportunity to have His way. Life began to change drastically for me. My desires were changing and I was growing in holiness. When you seek after righteousness you will indeed find it. My prayer life had now grown beyond just my time in the room by myself. I had joined the intercessory group at church. I now found myself praying through out the day.

In P.I.T. we were named after individuals in the bible and guess who I was named after?

Daniel, the Praying Prophet, I began to realize that when I pray for people God gives me revelation about them. There are secret things He will share which are meant for me to offer up back to him. I'm thankful for being an intercessor and being able to really get in my prayer closet to seek Gods wisdom not only for myself but also on behalf of others.

Also during this time I began to fast once per week, which I thought I would never survive when, I first started. When you combine reading the word, fasting and praying on a regular basis, you set yourself apart for God to use. Fasting brings about discipline and helps to keep things under submission. When you begin to fast, start out gradually with something you know you will stick with. Eventually you will grow and mature in it and be able to go for long periods of time.

Phases of Sanctification

Cognition - understanding the word is key to the sanctification process. If you are unclear what the scripture says about it then you can't follow the process. Ask God for revelation and attend classes so that you are clear about what your reading. This helps shape how you think. Once you are clear on the word and you make up your mind to really follow the word you become unmovable. The word helps to shape your convictions and at some point you get in to a place of no compromise no matter what the cost.

2 Corinthians 4:13-14 (CJB) The Tanakh says, "I trusted, therefore I spoke." Since we have that same Spirit who enables us to trust, we also trust and therefore speak; because we know that he who raised the Lord Yeshua will also raise us with Yeshua and bring us along with you into his presence.

Perfect Holiness (death)

In this stage of the process you die to sin, old self, old habits, old ways, etc. When you attend a funeral you see the physical body located in the casket but if you were to touch it, it wouldn't respond because it can't feel anything. When something is dead there is no movement or reaction to the environment. When you die to your flesh you are impenetrable and impervious to what's happening around you. You are only moving in the things of God. When Daniel was placed in the lions' den he had to die to his own fears and believe that he would not be harmed. When the solider requested that Jesus heal his daughter he had to die to doubt and believe that His word alone could heal her. When you die to old schools of thought you take on life because the word of the Lord is life in itself.

Revelation 19:8 says, fine linen, bright and clean has been given her to wear. Fine linen means the righteous deeds of God's people.

In death often times when the body is prepared for burial it's cleaned, patched up if necessary and then dressed in a fine outfit. People are generally dressed in some type of white outfit. Even in death we are presenting ourselves in a purified, righteous state.

On Monday, March 10, 2003, another prophetic word was given by Prophetess Maria Vaughn, which spoke to my prayer life.

The Lord would say to you "stay prayerful there have been many trials tests and tribulations that you have faced but it was prayer that brought you through those tests trials and tribulations. He told me to tell you to be strong in the Lord. Every time you open your mouth and lift up a prayer you are tearing satan's Kingdom to pieces. Remember he hates when you open your mouth, so why not destroy it with your weapon, "PRAYER". Be encouraged and be obedient to God's voice. Thus saith the Spirit of the Lord."

Here God was pointing out the importance of prayer and the effects that prayer has on the kingdom of darkness. So I make sure I use my weapon of prayer every chance I get.

LIVING A YIELDED LIFE

You would think that after all of this I would stay in a place with God but no just when you think you've died to the things you were a slave to, a test will come to show you exactly where you are. In 2005 I was in a place where I was reading the word daily, praying and really in full relationship with the Lord. However, I began having dreams about connecting with a significant other. There was nothing graphic, but one dream showed me two gold ropes separate and then they came together and intertwined to become one gold rope. This dream signified to me that I was getting ready to connect with someone and our bond would be so tight you really wouldn't be able to see where one begins and the other ends. Instead of me realizing that just because I saw it in my dreams didn't mean it was happening right then; I then proceeded to open myself up to the idea of dating someone.

The first person I met and considered

going to dinner with didn't even believe in God, which I didn't find out until we talked over dinner. What a mistake? He was great to talk to but only really good for one date. Since he had no relationship to God he definitely was not looking to entertain a non-sexual relationship. We communicated for a short period of time and then that ended. The next gentleman was someone who I was slightly familiar with but didn't know personally. We met and went on a few dates and I tried to work with him but still had reservations.

Things progressed and we hang out a few times and he asked to take me to meet some of his family in Maryland. Although, my red flags weren't raised, I observed my oldest son. When dating you should watch how your kids react to them. My son would always look at him so strange and when we went to Maryland he stood against the wall as soon as he entered the room and looked up in the ceiling. I then realized he could see spirits hovering around in the room but we were there and all I could do was pray.

We stayed for some time to fellowship with his people and went home. I asked my son why he looked at the gentleman like he did; I asked him did he not like him. My son said, "some times I do and some times I don't." From that point I was a little reserved even when the gentleman told me that my son was very observant of our relationship. The gentleman believed my son did not like him. A week or so went by and we hadn't hung out so when I chatted with him over the phone and he said I will stop by and see you tonight the Lord told me, "no don't do it" like a nut I said, "yes".

When your kids show signs that there is something wrong with the person you bring around them, moreover when you know your kids are prophetic, don't ignore that. Investigate into it because it's God trying to get your attention and he will use dreams, visions, spoken word, people, and even your kids. Don't be so focused that you are ignoring the signs that God is giving you. I'm thankful that I heard my son and really began to focus in to make sure this didn't continue. It wasn't long after this that this individual could no longer be around us and I'm thankful that the angels of the Lord saw to it that distance remained between us. Let God protect you from outsiders and yourself because often times we are our worst enemy.

You may simply want a companion but be sure the person you choose understands where you are and where your limits are. If you haven't come across someone who can respect that, then it's not going to work. It will either draw you out of the place you're in with God or it will cause you to separate from the individual. Set a standard for yourself and some boundaries that you aren't willing to cross so that when you meet someone and you make those things plain they will either honor that or they will leave. Learn to be all right either way and it will help you to not be in a place of loneliness. When you are lonely it will leave you open to entertain things you wouldn't normally.

After that episode, I stopped and said I will just remain alone. I threw myself in to my work and ministry and really made those two things outside of my children my whole life. God allowed me to see that just because I was separating myself for long periods of time like years in between it didn't mean that the desire had left me.

Throughout the next few years I would have similar tests to show me where I was which wasn't where I thought. You may not sleep with someone but you can do enough to where it's just as if you did. A truly yielded life sets standards and sticks to them no matter what. If you know your area of weakness then don't cater to it but you must overcome it. You may be asking how do you do that? If you know you can't handle male company past a certain time, then you cut it off earlier. If you know you are feeling lonely on a particular day then call your friends and hang out with them. You may not do these exact things but the point I'm making is to not act on your desires and don't place yourself in a position where you know you are vulnerable. Your challenge may not have been fornication but it was something that you dealt with and may still be dealing with. You know exactly what it is because it's that thing that you felt you were finished with but from time to time when you are tested you are shown that you are still susceptible to it. Each time you resist what you would prefer to do to what God has commanded you to do, you worship him. Your actions say God I love you more than this act that I want to commit.

DEIRDRE AVANT

Purity

Purity is defined as the condition or quality of being pure; freedom from anything that debases, contaminates, pollutes, etc.

1 Thessalonians 4:3-5 reads, What God wants is that you be holy, that you keep away from sexual immorality, that each of you know how to manage his sexual impulses in a holy and honorable manner, without giving in to lustful desires, like the pagans who don't know God.

As a single person living without sex can be a challenge. For some it's a huge challenge and for others they simply have their days. Religious thinking says it's in your dress, makeup and where you go. Early on, the church believed that in order to remain pure you shouldn't go to the movies, listen to secular music, wear red lipstick and the list goes on. The interesting thing about purity is it has nothing to do with any of that. Most people can live this way as long as they aren't dating someone. As they develop feelings and desire builds usually their will power diminishes. It's very rare for a couple to get married these days and they haven't slept together before they walked down the aisle. The world will let you know that they sleep with whomever they are dating. It is considered normal practice and they assume you are too "churchy" or too holy if you aren't doing it with yours.

In the church people are afraid to say they are engaged in premarital sex because they fear being judged and ridiculed. It's definitely not open season where you should do what you want but you should be able to discuss with your leader, mentor, or overseer regarding what you are going through As we all know the wages of sin are death but God definitely gave us the ability to repent which means to turn away. Thank goodness for forgiveness!

Married couples struggle with how far to go with sex even though they are married. There are so many opinions, that you really have to seek the Lord on what is right. Some will say anything goes once you're married and others will tell you that you should pray before sex and pray after sex. These are the two extremes and I believe the truth lies somewhere in the middle. When you possess the Holy Spirit, He will convict you when things aren't right regardless to whether you're married or not. Since I've been married and I've been single I know both sides of the coin and there are lines you can cross as a married couple that I don't believe God sanctions.

WHERE I AM TODAY

Today I live a pretty separate life, meaning things I used to do and places I used to go, I don't have the desire for now. I can say life is somewhat off balance because I've switched from some things only to pour myself in to work. Too much of anything can cause you to be off balance in life so be sure you have people around you who can help you do other things. I pray daily but not always the same way and not always at the same time. I used to beat myself up when I didn't pray at 5 a.m. Often times I'm praying throughout the day and this doesn't mean long drawn out prayers, it is literally a conversation with the Lord as if you were speaking to a human being. Prayer keeps me connected to God and allows the Holy Spirit to speak clearly to me because of the relationship that I now have through prayer with God.

There was a time when I did not pray at all because I felt I didn't know how to pray to God or was unworthy to come to Him. Don't allow the enemy to let you believe that you don't have a right to come to God just as you are, where you are. If you notice many of God's prophets, disciples, and apostles prayed for instructions, which should clue you in to how important it is to stay connected. When I don't pray because I'm rushed or my schedule is crazy I feel like something is missing out of my day. It's like waking up next to your husband but not saying good morning or I love you. I've incorporated this in to my daily living and I pray you do the same. It is vital that you are connected with God in this hour to be clear on what is Him and what isn't. The relationship I have with God through prayer has allowed me to experience the miraculous.

One instance in particular that I clearly remember, I was looking to purchase a home and so I contacted my realtor and gave her a list of homes that I wanted to see in my price range. We arrived at one home in Wilmington and what we saw in the picture and what the house actually looked like was completely different. Against better judgment we went inside the house and from there it didn't get any better. The house was extremely dark and in need of much repair. Really the listing agent shouldn't even have had this on the market. I told my agent that since we were there let's take a look because maybe I can just ask for a reduction in price and get the house repaired. We looked downstairs and then we proceeded upstairs and to our amazement it got even worse. The doors were off the hinges and there were holes in the walls not to mention the floor. We could only look in two rooms upstairs because of all the clothes piled in the floor behind one of the doors. We proceeded to the master bedroom and I couldn't get the door open. The realtor tried to open the door and as she proceeded to the door her foot sunk in a hole that none of us saw and she began to fall. I was too far away to just hurry and catch her and I didn't want to run to her because the floor was already weak so I prayed instantly and squatted down and extended my arms because everything in me wanted to catch her.

As soon as I prayed, I could literally see hands extend from me and rest under her stomach, which gently guided her down to the floor. Now I'm wondering if I saw what I saw and did what I see really happen. We walked outside the house and the realtor is extremely angry and calls her main office to leave a message for the listing agent and file a claim for her ankle. When she got off the phone, she informed me of course that I was not buying that house and it shouldn't even be on the market. She said, "now I'm catholic but it was something creepy about that house." Then she said, "While upstairs as I was falling I swear there were hands under my stomach gently guiding me down to the floor."

God confirmed the question in my head about whether it happened or not. That is just one instance but there are several more and I know through relationship with God, I will experience more. As I mentioned before, each week for years now I fast at least one day a week. When I first started it was the most difficult thing to do to deny myself food for hours. It was even more difficult to do it during work hours because of all the donuts, bagels, lunch meetings where food where food was brought in. Over time it became second nature to fast. I can go out with someone for lunch and not eat a thing while accompanying him or her.

My church calls for us to fast often, which, only strengthens my ability to do it. Fasting is one of the best ways to strengthen your discipline and it enables you to learn to deny yourself even when it's not convenient. There is a clarity that you have but not only that your ability to do deliverance work is enhanced because the word says in Mark 9:29, He said to them "This kind can come forth by nothing, but by prayer and fasting." This is part of my life on a weekly basis that I wouldn't trade for the world. Is it always easy to do it, no but it's always worth doing it.

Finally I read the word multiple days out of the week. It used to be daily but now it's at least four times a week and that's just being honest. What happens with me now is that God will give me a word or a scripture and I will look it up immediately regardless of where I am or what I'm doing because often times it is relevant to what is happening or what is going to happen. I enjoy reading the word because no matter how long ago it was written you can find scenarios in it that fit the situation you have right now. Only God can give a word that is relevant across many generations thousands of years later.

Revelation is key to understanding the mysteries of God. I may not have scriptures committed to memory but when I speak or when it's needed the scripture will come out of my mouth verbatim because of the Holy Spirit and I believe that is all that is necessary. Often times when I speak with someone or over the pulpit I will go back and look something up in the Bible. The word is written on my heart and the Holy Spirit will give me what I need to say when necessary. By all means read the word everyday but if you have not memorized scriptures it doesn't mean that you don't know the word. The daily walk with Christ can still be a struggle in some areas but not the same as when I first started. You can read, pray and fast regularly but the flesh will still desire things. Your mind will still go places that it should not but through discipline and great connections and strong spiritual parents you can and will continue on your path. Remember without holiness you will not see God and holiness is tied to purity and sanctification. Hebrews 12:14 *Keep pursuing shalom with everyone and the holiness without which no one will see the Lord.*

NOTES

1. www.dictionary.com

2. www.biblestudytools.com

3. http://www.biblicaltraining.org/library/sanctification-wayne-grudem

4. (http://www.soniclight.com/constable/notes/htm/OT/Leviticus/Leviticus.htm

5. (http://bible-truth.org/msg4.html)

ABOUT THE AUTHOR

Prophetess Deirdre Avant called, appointed, and anointed by God as a prophetess to the nations. She is the founder and president of the Deirdre Y. Avant Ministries. In order for her to be here, God allowed her to be born through Robert and Viola. This was always in the mind and the plan of God that He would order this woman of God's steps regarding ministry. She was called into the prophetic office in the summer of 2002 and acknowledged her calling in the fall of 2002.

Prophetess Deirdre Avant was properly birthed into the office and given impartation by her prophetic father, Prophet Raymond P. Stansbury of Wilmington, DE. Pastor of "Prophetic House of Truth Outreach" on Friday, May 14, 2003. She has attended an intense six-month course at The P.I.T. School of Ministry in 2003. God confirmed her calling into the office through dreams and visions.

After the confirmation of her calling she did the necessary things to enhance the prophetic that was in her. The devil thought that fornication and rebellion would have kept the mouth of this prophetess closed; even though that weapon was formed it did not come against her.

Gifted in administration and an accomplished coordinator, she is the CEO of Professional Administrative Services and the founder of Daughters of Zion, Inc. – a non-profit organization that ministers to young women dealing with foster care. She is a covenant member of New Destiny Fellowship, Wilmington, DE, under the covering of Bishop Thomas Wesley Weeks, Sr. where she functions as Intercessor, Altar Worker and Ministry Administrator.

Hobbies and Talents: She has operated in music ministry over the years between the Delaware, Maryland, and Virginia Area. She also enjoys volunteer work with children who have learning disabilities. It is Prophetess Avant's purpose to speak the true word of God, which will destroy the works of the devil. She is a single mom to Brandon and Arion. Her Pastoral father was the late Rev. Mack; her spiritual Mothers are Pastor Ward, Ms. Carolyn Graham, and Pastor Gamble.

What she really wants you to know is that she is a no-nonsense type of person. She wants people to be real with her. Lies and deceit are of the devil and they need to be put to rest. She is a woman of the truth and has no problems with standing up for the truth regardless of who is telling the lie.